Texas Divorce Survival Guide

How to Avoid Common Mistakes,
Pick the Right Lawyer
and Move on with Your Life

by David Todd

Legal disclaimer: I am not allowed to give legal advice in this book. The suggestions and the warnings I provide in this book are not a substitute for consulting with or hiring an attorney. Please remember that I cannot give you legal advice unless and until you hire me and I have agreed in writing to accept your case.

David Todd, Attorney at Law
Todd Law Firm, PLLC
3800 N. Lamar Blvd., Suite 200
Austin, Texas 78756
(512) 472-7799
davidtoddlaw.com

Dear Reader:

Thank you for reading this book. The fact that you are taking the time to educate yourself about Texas divorce shows that you are serious about getting a good result in your case. I hope this information helps you get the best possible outcome for your case so you can move on with your life!

- David Todd

This guide Includes:

* Divorce myths
* Common questions about divorce
* Issues to be decided in divorce
* How to improve the odds of winning your case
* Deadly mistakes that can destroy your case
* The truth about lawyer advertising
* How to resolve your case with less stress
* How to find a qualified divorce attorney

Note: Although this guide focuses mainly on divorce issues, much of the information also applies to modification of existing decrees, as well as custody cases (whether the child's parents are married or not).

Why did I write this guide?

Over the years in my practice, I have seen the types of pressure and scare tactics that are sometimes used in divorce by spouses and their attorneys. The information in this book should help you replace fear with knowledge and teach you how to avoid some of the most common pitfalls in getting divorced in Texas.

I believe it is to your benefit to learn the information in this book, at your own pace and without any pressure, before you talk to an attorney or sign anything. Once you become educated about how divorce works and about your rights, the less susceptible you will be to intimidation by your spouse or their lawyer. By being better informed, I believe you will make better decisions regarding your case and suffer less stress as you work through your divorce.

Ready? Let's dive into the nuts and bolts of Texas divorce and learn how you can avoid the most common mistakes and succeed in your case.

Deadly mistakes that can destroy your case

1. Waiting too long before seeking legal help.

Texas law requires that you follow certain procedures when you file for divorce, as well as if you receive notice that your spouse has filed for divorce. There are certain forms and procedures that must be used to file for divorce, respond when sued for divorce, and request information and documents from the other party. There are also certain deadlines you must meet. Missing these deadlines can be fatal to your case. Therefore, it is crucial that you contact an attorney as soon as possible.

2. Hiding your history (or that of your spouse or your children) from your attorney.

If you file for divorce, the opposing party has the right to obtain information from you regarding your financial, criminal, parental, substance abuse, medical and psychological history. Even if you do not give it to them voluntarily, they may be able to obtain it from other sources. If you hide or lie about any of these issues and it is discovered by the other side, your credibility is destroyed, and it will almost certainly damage your ability to get the outcome you want in your divorce. If you tell your attorney up front about all prior history, they can evaluate whether or not it will be a problem for your case. However, your attorney cannot deal with an issue about which he or she does not know.

3. Hiding assets.

The quickest way to lose the assets you are entitled to in a divorce is by trying to hide assets, debts, etc. from the other side or the court. Most spouses have a general idea about what assets exist in the marriage, so they may know when you are hiding something. Also, there are other ways for the opposing side to discover any assets that you do not disclose. You will usually get a reasonable division of assets if you are completely honest about your total financial situation. If you lie about it, you are inviting the court to punish you by giving your assets to your spouse.

4.   Not working as a team with your attorney

Although the attorney is in charge of preparing the case, he or she will need your help to do so. During the course of a divorce case, it is essential that your attorney be able to contact you and, when necessary, enlist your help in obtaining certain information and documents. You will also need to be available to assist your attorney by answering discovery requests (formal requests for documents and other information) from the other side, preparing for depositions and preparing for court hearings. The best attorney in the world cannot help you if you do not assist them in preparing your case.

5.   Misbehaving in court or at a deposition.

When you go to court or to a deposition the rules are simple: tell the truth, dress appropriately (nice, conservative clothing), be polite, do not get angry, do not answer a question that is not asked, do not argue with the judge or the opposing attorney, if you do not know the answer to a question do not guess, and do not talk over someone who is speaking.

Remember that when you go to trial, you are "Exhibit A". If the jury or the judge does not like you and does not believe you, they will look for a way to deny you what you are requesting, and you will lose. The way to be likable and believable is to assist your attorney in preparing ahead of time for your testimony, being completely honest at all times and being courteous to everyone involved in the case (yes, that even includes your spouse and their lawyer). If you are obnoxious or do not tell the truth in discovery, at deposition or at trial, you will damage your case. If the judge or jury likes you and believes your story, they will usually try to find a way to help you achieve the result you want, or at least a fair result. And, even if your case settles without a trial, being courteous and honest with the opposing side and their attorney will usually yield a better result and cause less stress for everyone, especially the children.

Myths: Common, false beliefs about Texas divorce

* If my spouse has an attorney, I do not need one.

* All divorce cases go to trial.

* If my spouse works and I do not, I will lose my share of the assets in a divorce.

* If my spouse works and I do not, or if I have ever been arrested or had a problem with drugs, alcohol or mental illness, I will lose custody of my children.

* I have to prove my spouse did something wrong in order to get a divorce.

* My spouse can control how much money I have to for legal fees and living expenses during the divorce.

* If my spouse worked outside the home during our marriage and I did not, I will not receive much of the assets.

* I do not need to take any steps to protect myself financially before starting the divorce process.

* I do not need to worry about emails, phone calls and social media postings during my divorce.

* All lawyers who handle divorce cases have the same experience and ability.

* If my spouse insists on settling the divorce, I have to agree.

* If I want to settle my case without going to court, I do not have to prepare for trial.

* There is never a good reason to take a divorce case to trial.

* Mediation is a waste of time.

* There is no need to plan for the post-divorce relationship with my spouse.

Reality:

Not every divorce case requires an attorney. If you have no children and little to no assets, you may not need to hire a lawyer. Otherwise, you probably need legal help with the process. This is especially true if you and your spouse cannot negotiate in a rational, calm manner regarding money, children or any other aspect of the divorce.

Even when you are able to negotiate rationally with your spouse, you may need an attorney to help you sort out the technical aspects of the divorce. If you have a large amount of assets to be divided, you may need the help of an attorney and possibly other professionals (such as an accountant) to help you in locating assets, determining their value and determining a fair division. If you cannot agree regarding where the children should live, the amount of child support to be paid, or the details of visitation schedules, you probably will need the help of an attorney.

If your spouse hires an attorney, it is important to remember that their attorney owes a duty of loyalty to them and not to you. There are many issues in divorce concerning asset division or child custody that can be ordered in a way that is more advantageous to one party than the other party. As long as what is being sought is legal and ethical, it is the duty of your spouse's attorney to gain that advantage for their client, if that is what the client wants.

When your marriage is ending, the goal of your spouse may be, quite simply, to settle the divorce while paying you the least amount of money and granting you the least favorable deal regarding your children. You should be suspicious of any settlement offer made to you by your spouse or their attorney unless you have it reviewed by your own attorney first. Even if the offer turns out to be fair and reasonable, you should have it reviewed by your own lawyer before you agree to it.

You should at least have a consultation with an attorney so that you understand your rights under Texas divorce law. This is especially true if you are being pressured to settle the case quickly under terms that your spouse or his attorney drafted. **Never sign anything without having your own attorney review it first!**

If the parties cannot agree on how the children will be cared for or how assets will be handled during the divorce process, a temporary orders hearing may be necessary. At this hearing both sides present evidence and the court then issues temporary orders that control the parties' behavior until the divorce is finalized by settlement or final trial. Temporary orders can be very important in setting a precedent for how the case will eventually be resolved. It often turns out to be the "trial" of the case so you should take it seriously and prepare for it.

Not all divorce cases go to final trial. Many divorces in Texas eventually settle by agreement of the parties, often with the help of a process called mediation. In mediation, a neutral third party tries to help you and your spouse reach a voluntary, mutually-agreeable settlement. After some work has been done to insure both parties understand what assets and debts exist, the status of the children and what the objectives of both spouses are in the divorce, mediation is often an excellent means of resolving the case without the necessity of having a trial. Most Texas courts require you to attend mediation before you are allowed to have a trial.

Usually the best divorce mediator is a family law attorney or former judge who mediates family law cases full time and understands the risks and costs of trial, and who can assess from their own experience the likely outcome of a trial in any given case.

The meditation process is voluntary in that no one can force you to accept a bad agreement. However, mediation is popular because it is usually better for the parties to come up with their own solution regarding asset division and child custody, rather than going to the time, expense and emotional stress of trying the case. It is usually better for the parties to decide what happens with their children and property rather than leave these decisions in the hands of a stranger (i.e. the judge or the jury) who knows nothing about your situation until the morning of trial.

Remember, judges and juries are people and no attorney can guarantee what they will decide in any given case.

Settling a case by agreement also lays the groundwork for an amicable post-divorce relationship between the parties. If a married couple has no children, and is simply dividing assets, they may choose never to deal with each other again after the divorce. However, if the couple has children, the parties are generally going to have to continue to deal with each other on issues related to child support, visitation, health, education, etc., until all the children have reached the age of 18 years and graduated high school. Therefore, to the extent the parties can reach a reasonable agreement and avoid an expensive and stressful court battle, they will generally have better feelings towards each other and have an easier time working together and communicating regarding child issues after the divorce. Children also benefit from seeing a constructive relationship between their parents, even if they are no longer married.

However, if you cannot arrive at a fair agreement with your spouse, Texas law does provide both parties with significant protections, and it is often worthwhile to take the case to trial rather than accepting a lopsided agreement.

Even though many cases settle without a trial, it is important that your attorney prepare your case from the very beginning as if it was going to trial. This approach ensures that, if the case does not settle, you will not be caught unprepared on the eve of a trial that will decide your future and the future of your children. Also, when both parties are prepared to go to trial, this usually means that both parties have received complete information and disclosure from the other side. Being prepared and fully informed allows you to negotiate from a position of strength. When you are prepared, you know what the issues are, what assets are to be divided and what child issues may come up during the trial. You also know the strengths and weaknesses of your case. This allows the parties to reach an agreement while feeling comfortable that they have complete knowledge of all the issues related to the divorce and that they are agreeing to something that is reasonable.

It is extremely dangerous to wait until you get close to a trial date before you prepare for trial, because you lose valuable preparation time and the opportunity to discover if there are any problems with your case or whether there are witnesses or other evidence that should be developed before time runs out. This is a reason it is a good idea to talk to a lawyer as early in this process as possible.

The leverage you have in a divorce is the fact that, if you do not settle, your attorney may get a better result at trial than your spouse is offering. If you attorney is unprepared for or afraid to go to court, you lose that leverage.

Just because one spouse works and the other does not (or at least does not work outside the home), that does not mean that the working spouse will receive the majority of the family's assets or will automatically be awarded custody of the children. Texas law considers a married couple to be a partnership. It is presumed that both parties contributed equally to the financial success (or failure) of the partnership during the course of the marriage, and that both parties are entitled to a "just and right" division of these community assets if the "partnership" breaks up. This is why Texas is referred to as a "community property" state.

With some exceptions, every dollar earned by either party from the date of the marriage until the date of the divorce is presumed under Texas law to be community property subject to division between the husband and wife. Unfortunately, the same is true of every dollar of debt taken on by either party during the marriage. This division can change if you can prove that one party behaved badly during the marriage (adultery, abuse, or "wasting" of assets, for example) but the initial presumption is that the assets should be divided in a "just and right" manner, which often means equally. It is the burden of a party claiming that some assets (such as inheritance, property owned before the marriage, etc.) are their separate property to prove so in court. It is also the burden of a party making a claim for reimbursement from the community estate to prove they are entitled to it.

It may be helpful to examine further the idea of a Texas marriage being like a business partnership in order to understand the concept of "community property". In business, if you discover that your partner is not contributing fairly to the success of the business, or you simply cannot agree on the best course of action in running the business, you probably would split up the partnership. However, unless specified by contract (in the marriage context, a prenuptial or postnuptial agreement), you usually are not entitled to more of the assets than the other partner. Texas law acknowledges that some partnerships simply do not succeed and that is the risk each party takes when they agree to combine forces (i.e. get married).

Under limited circumstances, the court may award **"spousal maintenance"** to one party. The guidelines on whether to award spousal maintenance and how much to award are somewhat vague. A party may be entitled to spousal maintenance if the parties have been married a certain length of time, or under other special circumstances related to the special needs of the receiving spouse or of a child of the marriage or based on certain criminal behavior of one of the spouses. Spousal maintenance is usually not a substantial amount and it only continues for a limited period. This means that it is very important, especially for a spouse that does not have a high-paying job, to obtain a complete and fair division of all assets at the time of divorce so they do not have to rely on spousal maintenance for assistance. This is especially true in a sizable estate where there is an allegation of wrongdoing or other grounds for an unequal division of assets or for spousal maintenance.

The fact that Texas is a **"community property"** state also means that your spouse is not allowed to cut you off financially in order to gain an advantage during the course of the divorce. Many times, the working spouse will threaten the nonworking spouse with financial ruin if they try to get a divorce or if they do not agree to the divorce terms the working spouse desires. In such a situation, if there are assets available, the court may order the working spouse to provide money to the nonworking spouse to help with legal fees and living expenses while the divorce is pending. The court also usually orders the spouse who has been paying the mortgage, utilities, insurance, etc. continue to do so until the divorce is final.

Although Texas courts will normally make a spouse who earns more money provide some money to the other party during the course of the divorce, this process can take some time. In the meantime, if your spouse has moved or hidden assets, or cut you off from sources of money, your life can become very difficult in the early stages of the divorce. Therefore, it is essential that you take steps to protect yourself financially when facing the prospect of a divorce. This may involve transferring some of the community assets into a different bank account that only you have access to, as well as removing your name from any credit cards or other instruments that could incur additional debt during the divorce. An attorney can be particularly helpful in advising you regarding how to protect yourself financially when you are facing the possibility of divorce.

Regarding child custody, the fact that only one spouse works outside the home does not mean that either spouse has an advantage in the court's determination of who should have primary custody over the children. The spouse who does not work outside the home (or who makes considerably less money than the other spouse) is still considered a full partner in the marriage and given equal consideration in deciding what to do with both assets and children. The guiding principle of the courts in determining where a child lives, who pays child support (and how much), etc., is "the best interest of the child". The fact that one spouse earns more money than the other is not a deciding factor in deciding where the child should live, especially since the spouse with whom the child does not live will usually be required to pay child support to the other party. All the circumstances of the parties and of the marriage are considered by Texas courts in determining what custody arrangement would be in the best interest of the child.

Similarly, the fact that you have ever been arrested or had a problem with drugs, alcohol or mental illness does not necessarily mean you will lose custody of your children. Texas law requires the court to look at all the circumstances of your case in determining what custody arrangement is in the best interest of the child. The court is interested in knowing if, despite any of the above problems, you are able to be a good, responsible parent and make sound decisions for your child. Many people who have dealt with substance abuse or mental health issues are able to achieve their desired custody arrangement either by agreement with the other party or by showing the court that you are a good parent. If you have dealt with these types of issues in the past, an attorney can help you evaluate the impact they may have on your case.

Remember that your discussions with your attorney are confidential by law so be honest and complete when discussing past problems with your lawyer. The worst time for your attorney to find out about a "skeleton in your closet" is from the witness stand during a hearing or at trial. It can kill your case.

In addition to being a "community property" asset division state, Texas is a **"no fault"** divorce state. This means that neither party has to have done anything wrong in order for someone to get a divorce. Any person in Texas can get a divorce if they choose to, and their spouse cannot prevent them from doing so. If someone has done something wrong, that can be alleged in the divorce in order to affect asset division and child custody determinations, but it is not necessary in order to get divorced.

A divorce is a civil lawsuit. As in any other civil lawsuit, all communications between you and the other party are fair game for court. This means that you should assume that any and all e-mails, social media postings, letters, telephone calls and even in-person conversations between you, your spouse or anyone else (except one-on-one communications with your lawyer) are being recorded and kept and may appear again as evidence in the courtroom during your divorce. Therefore, you should be extremely careful regarding what you communicate regarding any issues related to the divorce, and you should retain all communications you receive from your spouse or anyone else related to the divorce in case you need to provide them to your attorney.

"Social media" such as Twitter and Facebook can be very damaging to your case. Most people think these sites are harmless, fun way to stay in touch with friends. However, remember that anything that you or your family or friends post on these sites can be brought up in court regarding fault in the breakup of the marriage, your income regarding child support calculations, your assets or your suitability regarding placement of the child.

The Truth about Divorce

The decision to divorce is a traumatic event. You have decided to leave the person with whom you thought you would spend your life. There is disappointment, embarrassment, anger, guilt, sadness and confusion in large doses.

Sometimes you have to fight in the process of divorce in order to stand up for your rights. However, some of these fights result from ignorance of the divorce process. Not knowing how divorce works, the details of the legal process, your legal options and the likely outcome at trial can make people fight more than necessary because they are afraid they will get "taken" by their spouse if they don't.

While divorce is expensive, it does not have to bankrupt you and your spouse. How much a divorce costs depends on the attitude and objectives of both parties. The more you and your spouse can readily agree to reasonable terms for settlement, the more time you will save and legal expense you will avoid. Some cases are worth spending substantial legal fees to fight because there are substantial assets involved. When a couple owns a lot of property, a slight difference in how the property is divided can make a very large difference in how much money you receive. And, in cases where there is a disagreement regarding child custody, it may be worth spending money to fight for the arrangement that you think is best for your children.

Even "collaborative law" cases, which are intended to be less contentious, which normally have two attorneys and various other experts (forensic C.P.A.'s, counselors, etc.) can become extremely expensive. And, if you ever reach an impasse and have to go to court, you have to fire both of the collaborative attorneys and hire different attorneys in order to try the case, which increases costs even further.

Obviously, this puts tremendous emotional and financial strain on the husband and wife. And the children suffer, both emotionally and in terms of money spent in the divorce that could be used to help the kids with things like college tuition.

A tremendous amount of time, effort and money goes into preparing most divorce cases because the lawyers and their clients have to be ready for trial. This means gathering lots of documents, arranging witnesses, even taking sworn depositions of the various players. The divorce process often includes numerous preliminary hearings regarding temporary orders, protective orders, injunctions, etc.

And, for those whose cases actually go to trial, the costs skyrocket and the parties may get so mad at each other that it is very hard for them to deal with each other regarding the kids after it is all over. Given all of the above, the more you can work out by agreement, the more time and money you will save and the more aggravation you will avoid.

Common Questions about Divorce

Navigating your way through a divorce case can be confusing during what is often a stressful and emotional time in your life. Not knowing what to expect can make it even harder. The following are answers to frequently-asked questions about Texas divorce.

How much does a divorce cost?

It is important for you to understand that divorce is an expensive process. You may find it ironic that in the U.S. the average cost of getting divorced is the same as getting married: $30,000.00 (which also happens to be the average cost of a new car). It is not uncommon for divorces with large estates or extended custody battles to exceed $100,000.00 in legal fees per side. In the biggest divorce battles, clients may spend more than a million dollars each getting divorced.

The hourly rate billing system used by most family law attorneys can put the lawyer at odds with the client. The longer the process takes, the higher the cost for the client, and the more money for the lawyer, without necessarily improving the outcome of the case. Many clients hire an attorney with a minimum initial retainer that seems reasonable, only to be shocked at the overall cost as they must continually replenish the retainer as the case goes on.

Even worse, some clients run out of money during the process and the attorney has to withdraw from the case.

Then the client has to stop proceedings and find a new lawyer or accept an unfavorable offer from the other side just to end the case. With the fate of your children and your assets at stake, that is a terrible position to be in. It is far better to know what your case will cost you and to arrange how you will pay for it before you begin the process. Then you and your attorney can focus on what really matters: obtaining the best possible outcome as quickly and efficiently as possible.

Note: In an effort to bring certainty (and sanity) to the process, we have adopted fixed fees for divorce and family law matters. This allows clients to budget for their case up-front and avoid the open-ended, "sky's the limit" legal fees they may otherwise end up paying. Contact us at the Todd Law Firm if you would like more information.

Can I get a legal separation?

No. Although a legal separation is available and sometimes required in many states, there is no legal separation in Texas. If you need to protect your interests regarding your property or your children while separated from your spouse, you must file for divorce and obtain temporary orders and/or a temporary restraining order. Also, there is no requirement of obtaining "separated" status prior to filing for divorce.

What if one spouse does not want the divorce?

In Texas, if one spouse wants to be divorced, the divorce will be granted. Texas is a "no fault" divorce state, meaning fault does not have to be proven to obtain a divorce. Anyone who wants to get divorced in Texas, for any reason or no reason at all, may do so.

What if I am in a common-law marriage?

Common law marriage occurs when there has been no marriage license issued, but the law considers you married. Texas will find that you are "common law" married if you live together in the State of Texas, have a proven intent to be married, and hold yourselves out to others as husband and wife. There is no minimum time that you have to live together.

Living together and having children together does not automatically mean you are common law married under Texas law. The facts and circumstances of each case must be considered to determine whether a common law marriage exists.

If I am common law married, do I need to get divorced?

If you have been separated more than two years, then you do not need a divorce. Once you have been separated two years, the law presumes you were not common law married. If you have property to divide, the procedure to divide it will hinge on whether or not you are considered married under Texas law.

How long does it take to get divorced?

Texas has a minimum 60-day waiting period before a divorce can be finalized. The 60 days start running at the time the original petition for divorce is filed with the court. However, most divorces take longer than 60 days. While the average time to get divorced is about a year, the time frame for divorce may be anywhere from three to six months if it is agreed, and up to several years in a highly contested matter. The more agreements reached between you and your spouse as to the terms of the divorce, the sooner your divorce will be final.

It is almost always in the parties' best interest to resolve the case by agreement as quickly as possible in order avoid excessive legal fees and keep the time spent dealing with the divorce to a minimum.

This allows both parties to save more of their money, reduces the emotional stress and allows the parties to move on with their lives as quickly as possible. A quick resolution also may help lessen the trauma on the parties' children.

What is considered community property and community debt?

Texas is a "community property" state. In other words, all property owned by married persons on the dissolution of a marriage, whether by death or divorce, is presumed to be the property of both the husband and wife. Likewise, any debts incurred during marriage are presumed to be community debt. This means that the debts are presumed to be owed to creditors by both the husband and the wife. Like community property, community debt must also be divided in a divorce. However, since the creditor is not a party to the divorce action, the creditor may still pursue either spouse for collection of the debt (depending on the contract that created the debt), as creditors are not bound by the terms of the divorce decree and the divorce court's allocation of responsibility for joint debts. If the divorce court orders a spouse to pay a community debt and he or she does not, the other spouse may file an enforcement action against the non-paying spouse.

What is considered separate property?

Generally speaking, **"separate property"** is property acquired before a marriage and property acquired during marriage through gift or inheritance, or with funds that qualify as separate property. Also, married persons may agree in a properly drafted written agreement to **"partition"** community property, in which case that property becomes each spouse's separate property.

How does the court divide the property and debts?

Under the Texas Family Code, community property (both assets and debts) are supposed to be divided in a manner the court "deems just and right, having due regard for the rights of each party and any children of the marriage."

This does not mean that community property or debt must necessarily be equally divided. The judge dividing community property and debt may consider other factors, such as the size of your and your spouse's separate estates, any fault causing the divorce and reimbursement claims by a party's "separate estate" against the "community estate".

What happens at trial?

A trial is the final court hearing. All issues upon which the parties do not agree are presented to a judge or jury that will make a final decision. The issues are presented through testimony of the parties, witnesses, documents and other evidence presented to the court. If you have a "bench trial" (i.e. a judge but no jury) the judge decides both child and property issues. If you demand a jury, the jury has the final say on what happens with the property. The jury advises the court on what they believe should happen regarding the children, but the court has the final say regarding child issues.

When am I officially divorced?

You are divorced the moment the judge says so from the bench. Your divorce is considered final (for purposes of appeal) on the specific day the judge signs the final decree of divorce.

How soon can I remarry?

Since one of the parties may appeal a divorce within 30 days after the date it is final, you must wait a minimum of 30 days after your divorce decree is signed by the judge before you may get married again.

Nuts and Bolts: Basic Issues to Decide in Divorce

The issues that will be decided in your divorce are: what to do with property and what to do with children.

Property:

1. How to divide all the stuff you own, including automobiles, everything in the house, bank accounts, retirement accounts, the house, and personal items as well as who will take responsibility for paying which debts.

2. How to handle income taxes for the year before the divorce and the year of the divorce, what to do with

any tax refund and who gets tax deductions in the future.

3. Whether anyone is going to pay spousal maintenance and, if so, how much and for how long.

4. Whether the wife will go back to her previous name (maiden name or previous married name).

Children:

1. The rights and responsibilities of each parent regarding the children, including which parent determines the legal residence of the kids.

2. Whether the parent who determines the residence of the children (the **"primary"** parent) may move out of the area where the divorce occurred and take the children with them. This is called a **"geographic restriction"**.

3. When each parent will have the children (**"possession"**).

4. How much child support is to be paid.

Why, Why, Why? Grounds for Divorce

Lawyers do not encourage divorce any more than a doctor favors disease. It is a painful, life-altering experience for the spouses and their children. You should avoid it if reasonably possible. However, despite good intentions, some people just cannot (and should not) stay married.

If you are to divorce in Texas, you should know the grounds for divorce. Texas is a "no fault" divorce state. No one has to have done anything wrong in order for either spouse to get a divorce. Even if someone is at fault in the breakup of the marriage, you do not have to bring it up in order to divorce. Fault grounds include abandonment, adultery, conviction of a felony and cruel treatment.

In some cases, there is no reason to bring up any fault grounds for the divorce, even if they exist. If you insist on alleging fault, remember that your divorce may be longer and more expensive as a result. Always remember that your goal is to finish the divorce so your spouse's problems are no longer your problems.

In Texas, all that is necessary for divorce under the Texas Family Code is that "the marriage has become insupportable because of discord or conflict of personalities between husband and wife which has destroyed the legitimate ends of the marriage relationship and prevents any reasonable expectation of reconciliation." (This is also sometimes referred to as **"irreconcilable differences"**.) That simple statement will be in the Divorce Petition that is filed to start the divorce process. You will also be asked to confirm that statement as true when you "prove up" (finalize) your divorce before the judge. Whether you allege any other fault grounds is something you will determine after discussing your situation with your lawyer.

When, Where and Who? Jurisdiction and Venue

To file for divorce in Texas, one of the spouses has to have lived in Texas for the previous six months, and that person must have lived in the particular county where they file for divorce for at least 90 days. If you have recently moved counties, we will have to wait until you have lived in that county for 90 days if you want to file for divorce in that county.

Note that if your spouse lives outside Texas, they are not automatically subject to Texas jurisdiction. You have to establish that your spouse is subject to being divorced in a Texas court by living in Texas while married to you, or by meeting certain other **"long-arm jurisdiction"** requirements. Regardless, your spouse can always voluntarily submit to Texas jurisdiction by signing the legal papers in your divorce.

Chill Out: Keeping it Calm

There are a number of things you can do to avoid turning your divorce into a lengthy, expensive nightmare. The best way to keep the divorce calm and civilized is to avoid giving your spouse any reason to feel that you are going to take advantage of them.

Except to protect yourself as mentioned earlier, don't start taking money out of joint accounts. Don't cancel any health insurance or car insurance that your spouse uses. Don't cancel any credit cards your spouse uses. Don't remove items from safety deposit boxes. Don't take personal items out of the residence without the agreement of your spouse.

Not only will avoiding these types of behaviors help avoid aggravating the other side, it will keep you out of trouble with the judge.

A good rule of thumb before taking any action in your case is similar to the "Golden Rule". If a certain action by your spouse would make you feel upset or threatened, then do not do that action directed back at your spouse. This will keep your divorce as stress-free as possible and will save both you and your spouse considerable time and aggravation. Remember that you may have to explain any action you take to a judge later, so consult with your attorney to make sure you that what you are planning won't get you in trouble in court.

Keep It Real: Honesty in the Divorce Process

If you want a good outcome in your divorce, you need to commit up front to being straightforward and honest with your spouse. If you hide assets or lie about your earnings or account balances, you will end up with a lengthy, painful and expensive fight with your spouse. Remember: always consider how you would react if your spouse did the same to you. And, if the court catches you "lyin', cheatin' or stealin'", you may face contempt charges, fines and possibly even jail time.

Trust me on this one. **It does not pay to lie in a divorce.** Be honest about assets and income and get the divorce over with so you can begin your new life as soon as possible and without spending everything you have. Some people refer to the assets you have to give up to your spouse as the **"divorce tax"**. It is far better to just pay it and then rebuild your assets after the divorce than to wear both of you out fighting to get a little more of the "stuff" than your spouse gets.

Spyin', Lyin' and Cheatin': Forget the Surveillance

Following certain guidelines will help you achieve a good result in your divorce. Don't hide assets. Don't spy on your spouse, either electronically or otherwise. Don't record your spouse's phone calls to other people. Don't use "spyware" to track your spouse's email or computer use, and don't open your spouse's mail or email (all of which may violate state and federal criminal laws and land you in jail). Don't hide documents. Don't pull out hard drives to research your spouse's computer.

If you and your spouse are going to do an agreed divorce, you do not need any of the things mentioned above. You would only need those things if you want to have a trial and use those things as evidence of fault in the breakup of the marriage, etc. When you are going to do an agreed divorce, there is no need to focus on bad behavior by your spouse. Things like adultery, drug use, alcohol use, wasting of money, etc. are not important if you and your spouse can agree to a settlement that protects you both and the children. What is important is focusing on the terms of settlement. If there is a need to place restrictions on a parent drinking within a certain time before possessing the children, for example, that can be done. However, other than such common-sense restrictions, focusing on the past is unnecessary and counterproductive in most divorces.

If hiring a private detective, forensic computer expert or other professional become necessary in a case, discuss these actions with your attorney so they can advise and assist you in the process.

The Stuff: Property Issues in Texas Divorce

Puttin' It Away: Retirement Accounts

When you are dividing up financial accounts in a divorce, you need to treat retirement accounts differently from regular accounts. A regular IRA, 401(K), 403(B) or other retirement account requires that you reach a certain age if you want to withdraw the money without paying an early withdrawal penalty. Also, you will pay income tax on the withdrawals (unless it is a Roth IRA account). Money in a checking account has none of these restrictions, so every dollar in a checking account is effectively worth more than a dollar in a retirement account. The flip side is that retirement accounts can compound tax-deferred until the money is withdrawn and your income tax rate in retirement (when you withdraw the money) will usually be lower than while you are working.

Deciding how much less a dollar in a retirement account is worth than a dollar in a checking account is tricky because you have to make assumptions about your tax rate now and at retirement age, etc. Your tax professional can help with trying to set a value on a retirement account dollar versus those in a regular account. Some people simply choose to assume that a dollar in a retirement account is worth 25% of a dollar in a regular account because of these restrictions.

A better way to deal with this difference, if possible, is to divide retirement accounts separately from nonretirement accounts, so you are not comparing apples to oranges.

The Gold Watch: Pensions

Although most people today depend on the retirement accounts mentioned above ("defined contribution" accounts) some companies and governmental entities still offer pensions ("defined benefit" accounts). The value of a pension in a divorce depends on the person's years with the company at retirement, the person's age at retirement, the person's earnings at the time they retire, and a calculation of present value using an assumed interest rate from the time of the divorce until the time of retirement. Obviously, this can get complicated.

One practical way to divide a pension is to divide it at the time of the divorce using a "time" formula. You use the number of months the person retiring worked with the company, the number of months the couple were married and the asset distribution percentage you are using to divide the community estate.

For example: If the husband starts working at his company in 1985, gets married in 1990, gets divorced in 1995, the couple agrees at divorce that they will split the community estate 50% each, and the husband actually retires in 2020, the formula is as follows. The husband worked for the company for 35 years, or 420 months. The husband and wife were married 5 years, or 60 months. The portion of the pension that is community property is 60/420 = 14.285714%. The wife gets 50% of that 14.285714%, or 7.142857%. If the husband's monthly pension payment upon retirement is $1,000.00, then the wife will receive $71.43 per month (rounded up).

Obviously, this assumes that the pension plan still exists when the husband retires (i.e. the company has not gone bankrupt or applied for and received permission from the federal government to cancel the pension plan). It also assumes the husband does not quit or get fired before the pension vests. If any of the above occurs, both parties receive nothing. Also, if the wife dies before the husband retires, she (or more accurately, her estate) receives nothing. And many plans stop payments to the wife when the husband dies.

Using the formula above is often the best, most practical way to divide a pension in a divorce.

Splittin' the Retirement Loot: QDRO's

Often, retirement account assets must be shifted from one spouse to the other in the divorce. Moving money from one party's IRA account to the other party's IRA account can be as easy as sending a certified copy of the divorce decree to the brokerage firm or bank where the IRA is held and they will transfer the funds.

Dividing other retirement accounts, such as 401K plans or pensions, requires a Qualified Domestic Relations Order (for simplicity, lawyers and judges just call these a "QDRO", pronounced "kwadro"). QDRO preparation can be time-consuming, and the form required by each firm managing these types of accounts is different and the process sometimes involves altering and resubmitting the form more than once until the management firm accepts it.

If a pension is divided, there are two pensions created (the original and the new one benefiting the spouse). Dividing a 401K creates a new IRA in the name of the spouse. There should be no immediate penalties or taxes from this shift of assets. All the rules regarding penalties for early withdrawal, vesting requirements (for pensions), and taxes on money once you start to withdraw it, apply to the new account created the same as they apply to the original account. If the employee will pay taxes on pension benefits or 401K withdrawals, so will the ex-spouse. If the employee would be penalized for early withdrawal, so will the ex-spouse.

What's Yours and Mine: Property Division

If you and your spouse reach an agreement on your divorce and present it to the court in an agreed decree, the court will usually approve it without reviewing the property division to see if it is fair. This means you and your spouse can divide your property any way you want by agreement.

What happens if you cannot reach an agreement on how to divide property? At trial, the court will divide the **community property** in a "just and right" manner, which means pretty much whatever the court thinks it means (although in the vast majority of cases the property gets divided somewhere from a 50/50 to a 60/40 or a 70/30 split). The law presumes that everything you and your spouse have at the time of divorce is community property. Community property means that each item of property belongs both 100% to you and 100% to your spouse.

If you claim that something is your **separate property**, it is your burden to prove (via paperwork and/or testimony) that you either owned the item prior to the marriage or that you received it during the marriage by gift or inheritance. If you commingle separate property funds in an account with community property funds, it is your burden to prove how much of the account is separate property. The court removes the separate property from the estate and then decides how to divide what remains, which is the community property. To protect yourself and your future, it is essential to make sure your spouse is not trying to classify something as separate property that should be community property under the law.

Dividing the community estate can be tricky since earnings contributed to an account during the marriage, dividends, and income from rent are all community property. You can hire a forensic accountant to determine what is community and what is separate, which can be expensive and time-consuming.

To achieve a reasonable divorce, most couples use a simple method to determine what is community property and what is separate property. They assume that the value of the account at the time of the marriage is the separate property amount, and the difference between that initial value and the value at the time of the divorce is the community property amount. They then divide that community property amount. Many times, if both spouses have accounts that are of similar amounts (401K accounts, for example) the will just agree to each keep their own account and avoid the hassle of dividing them.

Once the court determines what is community property, it divides it in a "just and right" manner. Splitting this property equally between the parties (50/50) is a good starting point for the court. Deviating from this even split can be done for a number of reasons, including different earning capacities of the two parties, who will be raising the children after the divorce, or one party having much more separate property than the other, or fault in the breakup of the marriage.

Courts will sometimes divide the community property 60/40 for the reasons listed above, but that is usually the furthest most courts will deviate from 50/50 division. Exceptions where a court will give more than a 60/40 split (70/30, etc.) may occur where there is exceptionally bad behavior by one of the spouses (including adultery and hiding or wasting of assets). Courts rarely go beyond a 60/40 split since doing so makes their ruling more vulnerable to being overturned on an appeal filed by the "shortchanged" party.

To avoid all the complicated steps listed above, it is often better for the spouses to agree on a property split and present the court with an agreed divorce decree to sign.

40 Acres and a Mule: Real Estate

The home is, for most people, the largest asset in a divorce. The two common options for dealing with the home are to either sell the home and divide the proceeds, or for one party to keep the home. It is usually not recommended to keep the house with both parties as owners since this usually leads to future conflict over the house (whether and when and for how much to sell it, or how to handle repairs, etc.) It is much better to completely separate all community property so the parties never have to deal with each other on those issues again.

If you decide to sell the home, understand that it may not sell by the time the divorce is finalized. This can be the result of the time required to list and sell the house, a decision to wait to sell to see if market conditions improve, deciding to wait until the youngest child graduates high school, etc. You will want to include in your divorce decree language regarding who will live in the home until it sells, how to reimburse whoever invests money in the home for repairs or improvements, how the proceeds will be divided, what the deadline is for selling (or at least listing) the house (or other "trigger" events that will force the house to be sold), and who pays the mortgage, utilities and repairs in the meantime.

It often is simpler to have one party keep the home. However, you must decide how to "pay out" to the spouse that leaves the home their portion of the equity (if any) in the home. You can trade other assets for that portion of the equity, if there are enough other assets to do so. Otherwise, you must determine how much to pay out to the person who is leaving and where the money will come from. You also must decide what occurs if the person remaining in the home fails to make the mortgage or tax payments on the home.

A simple way to determine the "payout" is to have the house appraised, subtract the remaining mortgage amount and divide the remaining amount (the home equity) by two and give the departing spouse that much money. Remember that closing costs are usually around 8% (assuming the house is ever sold) so you may wish to subtract that amount from projected sales proceeds before determining the payout for the departing spouse. This also means that the party keeping the house will benefit or suffer in a future sale depending on what happens with home prices in the future.

If one party is to keep the house, you will need a Special Warranty Deed, in which the departing spouse gives the remaining spouse all their ownership rights to the house. You will also need a Deed of Trust to Secure Assumption, which is a guarantee by the remaining spouse to make the mortgage and tax payments, and which gives the departing spouse some protection if the remaining spouse fails to make those payments. If both spouses' names are on the mortgage, the departing spouse needs to be comfortable that the remaining spouse will make the mortgage payments because, even though the departing spouse no longer has an ownership interest in the house, the departing spouse could be sued and/or have their credit ruined if the remaining spouse fails to make the mortgage payments.

Another option is to refinance the house and remove the departing spouse's name from the mortgage. Sometimes you can borrow additional money in the refinance loan to use to pay out the departing spouse.
Remember that refinancing costs money, and the amount of equity in the home and the market (interest rate) conditions determine whether refinancing is worthwhile or even possible. Many decrees will include a deadline by which the remaining spouse must either refinance or sell the home.

Keep in mind that, if the parties are unable to agree on what to do with the house, courts will often simply order that the home be sold and that the proceeds, after all expenses are paid, are split between the parties.

You Owe, Big Time: Other Debt

Although the parties or the court in a divorce will divide up debt, remember that debt is controlled by contract law. That means that, regardless of what it says in the divorce decree concerning who will pay credit card bills, medical bills, student loans, etc., the creditor can and will sue the person whose name is on those bills, and the creditor is not bound by whatever is put in a divorce decree.

Usually the decree states that if a person takes an asset on which money is owed, that same person takes the debt. For example, if you are taking the house and a car, you also assume the debt on both of those items.

The decree normally says that each party will take all other debt (unsecured by any property) that is in that person's name. For any of the debt that is in your name but that was used to benefit both of you, you should try to offset half that debt amount with other property in order to make the property division fair to both parties.

What's in the Vault? Bank Accounts

To be enforceable, the divorce decree has to be specific about who gets what. If the decree said that a party receives "half the bank accounts", ambiguity may lead to conflict and a trip back to court to clarify the decree.

Sometimes the decree will order the parties to close all joint accounts and transfer the money into separate accounts for each party. Other times the decree will simply state that each party keeps the bank accounts that are in their own name. This second option avoids the need to specify in the divorce decree (which is a public document) that you have funds in a certain account at a certain bank.

Grandma's Napkin Rings: Dividing Miscellaneous, Personal Property

It is surprising how often dividing the personal items, rather than the big-ticket items like cash and retirement accounts, is what causes the most controversy in a divorce. Understand that courts have no interest in determining the value of the stuff in the house. Also remember that the only value a court would put on any item (and you should, too) is what it might sell for at a garage sale, today. If you cannot agree on how to divide these items, the court may order the parties to create an agreed list of those items. Then, after a coin toss to see who goes first, the court will allow one party to pick an item, then allow the other party to pick an item, and so on until every item has been chosen.

The old saw about dividing personal items is that, if the parties cannot agree on how to divide them, the judge will order that all this junk be put in a giant bag, smashed with a hammer, and divided by weight. Although it is a joke, it accurately reflects how uninterested most judges are in deciding who gets what items of personal property in a divorce.

One method to divide personal items is to create two lists: one list is items the wife is to get, the other list is items the husband is to get. Each list should just contain the name of the item without any information on estimated value, where or when it was bought or received, etc. If each party creates these lists, the attorneys may be able to assist the parties in agreeing on a final version of who gets which item.

Usually, if the parties have been separated for a while, much of the personal property items have already been separated. If that is the case, the final divorce decree will award each party the items currently in their possession and list any specific items that still need to be exchanged that are currently in the possession of the other spouse.

Laying It Out: Discovery; Inventory and Appraisement

"Discovery" is the formal, legal process of exchanging information between the parties in order to prepare for trial or facilitate reaching a settlement. Types of discovery include: **interrogatories** (written questions), requests for **disclosure**, requests for **production** and requests for **admission**. Discovery rules are designed to allow both parties to find out all relevant information related to the case prior to trial so that there are no major surprises.

Note that the discovery tool used most often in divorce cases is the Inventory and Appraisement ("I & A"). Each party fills out, signs and has notarized this form listing all the assets and debts of which they are aware. The parties then exchange these forms. If it is later discovered that a party was hiding something, they can face contempt of court and risk being sued by the opposing party. As with all other aspects of divorce, you need to be completely honest in answering discovery and filling out an inventory.

Render unto Caesar: Income Taxes

There are various ways to handle your taxes for the year of your divorce and for the previous year. Starting with the year in which you get married, you may either file as "married filing jointly" or you may file as "married filing separately". Your marital status for a certain year is determined by your status (married or divorced) on December 31 of that year.

For the year in which you divorce, you will have to file separately. For tax purposes, you pretend that you were divorced for that entire year. However, you must consider who will pay the taxes for the previous year (if not already paid): one party could pay it all, the parties could each pay half, or you could come up with a division based on how much each party earned.

You also have to determine who gets the tax refund, if any, or how it will be split. You also must determine who claims any mortgage interest payment deduction, as well as any tax credit for children.

Your attorney can advise you but should also consult your tax professional regarding these issues before you sign your divorce decree.

Even It Up: Judgment to Equalize Property Division

In trying to equalize property division in divorce, sometimes the parties have to resort to a promise by one party to pay a sum of money to the other party. In a divorce decree, this is called a judgment to equalize property division. If the spouse ordered to pay does not do so, the other party can get an abstract of judgment from the court clerk and record it with the county property records. This makes it very difficult for the other party to borrow money until they pay off the debt.

Remember, however, that you "cannot get blood from a stone". In other words, the judgment only helps if the party who owes you still has some "non-exempt" property of value that could be seized. Also, remember that a judgment could be wiped out in a bankruptcy.

Because of this, you should always try to get "money up front" (when the divorce is finalized) instead of a promise of future payment.

The Gift That Keeps on Giving: Alimony

There are two types of Alimony in Texas. The first type of alimony is **"contractual alimony".** This alimony can only be created by agreement of the parties (the court cannot order it). The parties agree on whatever amount they want each payment to be and whatever duration they want the payments to continue. The payments can be arranged to be paid directly to the ex-spouse or to be paid on behalf of the ex-spouse (to make mortgage payments, for example).

Contractual Alimony requires an **Agreement Incident to Divorce**, which is separate from the decree. Contractual alimony payments are often tax deductible for the person paying and taxable for the person receiving, but you must check with a tax professional regarding your particular situation.

The second type of alimony is **"statutory alimony"** (sometimes called "spousal maintenance"). It can be created by agreement of the parties or ordered by the court, and the payments are made directly to the receiving party. Factors that can create eligibility to request spousal maintenance include: criminal actions of a spouse, the length of the marriage, and the ability of a spouse to support himself or herself. You should discuss the details of your marriage with your attorney to determine your eligibility to request spousal maintenance and the amount and length of maintenance you might be awarded by the court.

Statutory alimony is designed to help someone "get back on their feet" financially (i.e. back into the work force and able to support themselves) via rehabilitation or training. Courts do not order it automatically, and the court usually wants to know specifically how the receiving party intends to use the funds to get back into the work force (additional schooling, renewing a particular vocational license, etc.). Statutory alimony is not intended to allow someone to avoid having to work. The court will only order statutory alimony (if any) for the amount and for the time period required to facilitate a spouse's plan to get back into the workforce to earn a living.

What'd You Call Me? Changing Your Name

A wife who took that last name of her current husband may, at the time of the divorce, change her name back to a name she has used before (her maiden name or a name used in a previous marriage) without having to pay any extra fee. If the wife wants to change her name to one she has never used before (including a different arrangement (order) of the names used before), this requires a separate lawsuit. Also, if a wife does not change her name at the time of the divorce, but later decides to do so, she will have to file a separate lawsuit and pay an additional court fee.

The husband cannot force the wife to stop using his last name. The decision to change her name is the wife's choice alone. Any woman contemplating a name change at the time of divorce must also decide if the change would result in her name being different from that of her children, and whether or not that matters enough to her to not change it.

Children in Texas Divorce

Kids "R" Us: More Child Issues

If you have children with your current spouse that are 18 years old, then they are adults under the Texas Family Code that are not dealt with in divorce, unless they are still enrolled in high school in which case support obligations may continue until they graduate.

If your child is an adult with a disability that will require continuing support, the support obligation may continue beyond age 18.

Any child you have had with someone other than your spouse is not part of the current divorce proceedings. A court-ordered obligation to support that other child, however, may affect your support amount in your current divorce case.

If you or your spouse have adopted a child, they are part of the current divorce proceeding.

If the wife in a divorce is pregnant, the court will not finalize the divorce until the child is born alive or has miscarried. The reason for this is to avoid the birth of a child after the divorce for which no support and custody have been arranged. The exception to this is where the husband and wife agree that the unborn child is not the child of the husband. If you two do not agree regarding this issue, you may have to wait until the child is born and the child and husband will have to submit to DNA paternity testing.

There are only two things involved in any divorce – the "stuff" (property), and the kids. If you have children, you probably will agree that what happens with them is more important, and can lead to bigger arguments, than what happens with the "stuff".

In most cases it is preferable that you and your spouse come to an agreement regarding what to do with your children. If you don't, you will end up going to trial on that issue, which will be stressful, more expensive, and can sour your post-divorce relationship with your spouse. And the trial process is almost always harmful to the children. In most cases, after all the drama and stress of a trial, the court is going to order some type of joint custody for you both and order you to work together regarding kid issues anyway. So, why not avoid all that pain and jump ahead to the same result by agreement? The two of you will have to communicate and work together to some extent regarding the children until they all reach age 18 and graduate from high school anyway, so the sooner you can start working together for their benefit, the better.

In some cases, of course, the parties simply cannot agree on what is best for the children and they must have a judge or jury make that decision for them.

Obviously, if communication between you and your spouse was smooth and you agreed regarding child-rearing issues, you might not be getting divorced at all. Since kid issues can be very emotional, a good counselor can often help you both learn how to work together for the children's benefit, even though the marriage is ending. While your lawyer can empathize with what you are going through, they are not a replacement for a good therapist. It may be best to use a therapist that has not been counseling either of you individually so that your spouse feels comfortable that the counselor is "neutral" in their loyalties. Explain to the counselor that you are not there to "fix" the marriage, but rather to learn how to work together regarding the children, even after the divorce.

If You Can't Say Anything Nice: Protecting the Children

During your divorce, it is essential that you not "bad mouth" your spouse in any situation where your children might hear it. Who is the "good guy" or "bad guy" in the divorce is irrelevant if you want to get divorced with the minimum trauma to your children. Remember that you chose your spouse, but your children did not choose their parents. Regardless of who is the "better" parent, or who is to blame for the divorce, your children need to feel free and encouraged to love and respect both parents during and after the divorce. And if you trash the other parent to a child, you put them in a position to choose sides, which is harmful to the child (and remember, they might not choose you!).

Any problems your spouse has will become apparent to your child when they are old enough, without you telling them or trying to influence them. Also, courts really dislike it when you put your kids in the middle of your divorce, and your case will suffer if the court catches you doing it.

Also, if you drag your kids into the middle of the divorce, you guarantee that you will have an expensive, lengthy and ugly custody fight, in which you and your kids will both suffer.

Remember, keep it civil, and keep the kids out of it to save yourself time, money and aggravation.

Leave 'Em Out of This: Taking Care of the Kids

During your divorce, it is very important to not place your children in the middle of the process. An important way to do this is to avoid using your kids to deliver messages to your spouse.

Even if your child delivers the message correctly (doubtful in many cases) it places the child between you and your spouse, a very uncomfortable place for a child during a divorce.

Most courts will hold it against you if you use your kids to relay messages. Some courts even have standing orders that prohibit divorcing parties from doing this. Many courts will order the parties to attend divorce parenting classes which address this issue as well as many other issues divorcing couples face regarding their children. Even if not ordered by the court, it is recommended that you and your spouse attend one of these courses as they are cheap, convenient and usually very helpful.

Always communicate directly with your spouse, or if necessary communicate through the attorneys. Leave the children out of it. Your divorce will go much more smoothly and your kids will be much happier.

What's It All Mean? Custody vs. Possession vs. Conservatorship

Many people confuse these terms. While many people use the term **"custody"** loosely to describe the arrangement between former spouses and their kids, the Texas Family Code and family lawyers and judges do not use this term.

"Possession" simply means the right to have the child with you. **"Conservatorship"** means all of the rights and duties of both parents regarding a child, such as determining where the child lives, receiving or paying child support, making decisions or giving consent for the child regarding marriage, joining the military, medical issues and educational issues.

Out with the Old, In with the New: Conservatorship

You may have heard the terms **"sole managing conservator"** and **"possessory conservator"**. These are the old terms that used to be used in Texas family law. Back then, the sole managing conservator (often the mother) had the right to make all the real decisions regarding the child, the child lived with them, and they collected child support from the possessory conservator (usually the father), who had the right to have possession of the child at certain times. The rights possessed by the parties were specifically laid out depending on whether they were the sole managing conservator or the possessory conservator.

The Texas legislature changed the Texas Family Code and, for the most part, did away with the terms sole managing conservator and possessory conservator. The legislature set up a new arrangement called **"joint managing conservatorship",** which, unless you present convincing evidence otherwise (or the parties agree to use the old arrangement instead), is presumed to be in the best interest of the child (and that means joint managing conservatorship is what the court will order in your case). Joint managing conservatorship is much more flexible than the old system, because the parties can agree on how to divide up, or share, the various rights regarding the child, and it can be made to be as restrictive as the old sole possessory conservatorship if the evidence at trial warrants it (or if the parties agree to do that).

Most divorce cases result in a joint managing conservatorship of the children. All the rights regarding your child will be laid out, and either you and your spouse will have to agree on how to divide up or share each of these rights, or the court will decide for you.

Many of the rights can be shared, such as the right to take the child for medical treatment when they are injured or ill while in your possession, or the right to attend school and extracurricular activities. Other rights have various options, such as the right to consent to your child joining the military when they turn 17 years old. In this example, you could agree that either party can consent, or you can require the both parties must consent in order for it to happen.

The right that cannot be shared is the right to designate the primary residence of the child. This will be the address the child gives to his school and also determines their school district. As verbal shorthand, courts will sometimes refer to this party as the **"primary"** conservator. If there is a fight regarding children in a Texas divorce, it is often regarding whom should be the primary conservator with this residency right.

Note that the Texas Family Code does not favor the mother over the father, or vice-versa, as to who should be the "primary" conservator. However, all things being equal (both mom and dad are good parents with no serious substance abuse, child neglect or psychological issues) Texas courts seem to name the mother as the primary more often than the father, especially if the child is very young. This is unfortunate for the dad. If he really wants to go to court to try and get the child ordered to live with him (over the mother's objection) he can, but it is usually an uphill battle.

The party with this right also has the right to receive **child support**, regardless of whatever possession schedule you come up with (even equal time with the child). Remember that child support and possession are completely separate issues, both at the time of the divorce and for the remainder of the time your child is a minor. You cannot stop paying your court-ordered child support simply because the other party denies you your court-ordered possession time, and you cannot deny possession time due to failure to pay child support. If either of these problems arises down the road, the remedy is to ask the court to enforce the orders. You can, of course, agree to no child support being paid by either party if you wish, and spell that out in your agreed order.

If the right to designate residency is a "hot button" issue in your case, you can agree that neither party has that right, but that the residence of one of the spouses (agreed to between you and the other party) determines the residence of the child. This may sound like silly "hair splitting" but it can sometimes be a solution that prevents one party from "losing face" by not being named the primary joint managing conservator (since neither party is named primary). Remember, the goal is to get the divorce done, so if using this type of language helps resolve the divorce, use it.

Your Time's Comin': Possession

"Possession" refers to the rights of the "non-primary" conservator (remember that the "primary" conservator is the one who determines the child's legal residence) to have the child with them at certain times. The first thing to remember is that the parties are always free to deviate, by agreement, from the possession order in the divorce decree. The best post-divorce relationships use this informal approach quite often, with both sides being flexible for the benefit of the children. The possession order is there as a "safety net" in case you don't agree regarding a particular weekend, for example. The possession order gives everyone notice regarding who has the child and when.

In most cases it is easiest and best to follow the Texas Standard Possession Order in the Texas Family Code for several reasons. First, courts like it, are familiar with it and will often make you use it if you don't agree to something different.

Second, child development experts think that this type of possession schedule is better for the kids than any kind of "week on, week off" schedule. This is another reason why courts like to order standard possession.

Third, standard possession is well laid-out, battle-tested in thousands of divorces and provides predictability to the parents and the children.

You can agree to something different, but setting up your own, strange possession arrangement often leads to different interpretations and can buy you a trip back to court to fight about those terms in the future.

The **Texas Standard Possession Schedule** is lengthy and detailed, but the main points are as follows.

1. The primary conservator is the default, meaning the child is with them at all times not reserved for the other party in the Standard Possession Order;
2. The non-primary conservator has the child the 1st, 3rd and 5th weekend of every month, starting on Friday at 6 p.m. (this can be changed to the time when school lets out) and ending on Sunday at 6 p.m. (this can be extended by agreement to when school begins on Monday morning);
3. Thursday evenings during the school year (this can be changed to start when school ends on Thursday to end when school resumes on Friday);
4. 30 days in the summer;
5. Christmas from when school lets out for the holiday until December 28 at noon (then with the other party until school resumes). The next year, the Christmas schedule reverses.
6. Thanksgiving alternates between the parties each year.

For children under 3 years old, many courts use a "stair step" possession schedule that gradually increases time the child spends with the non-primary conservator until arriving at Standard Possession at age 3.

When the child reaches age 12 they can let the court know (in a proceeding to modify the possession order) if they want to go live with the other parent. The court does not have to follow the child's wishes but will take those wishes into account in any court proceeding where the non-primary conservator wants to have the child come live with them.

When a child reaches age 15, and especially if they have a car and a license, it is difficult to make them follow the Standard Possession Order. In light of this, some parents place a provision in the decree that once the child reaches age 15, the child can spend any time with the non-primary conservator that is agreed to by the non-primary conservator and the child.

If either party wants it, a court will usually include a **"morality clause"** which is language prohibiting either party from having an unrelated adult of the opposite sex in the house between (for example) 10 p.m. and 8 a.m. when that parent is in possession of the child. This also applies to vacation time with the children, regardless the fact that you are away from the "house".

Live Wherever You Want, as Long as It's Here: Domicile Restriction

Domicile restriction was born out of the concern by the "non-primary" joint managing conservator (the one who has a visitation schedule with the child and pays child support) that the other party will move so far away with the child that visitation will be difficult or impossible.

Some courts impose these restrictions routinely. Other courts will usually impose one if requested. The restrictions are usually to a certain county, or a certain county and contiguous counties (meaning all the counties whose borders "touch" the main county). You can make the restriction narrower (a particular school district, for example) or broader (the entire state of Texas).

Although some couples agree not to require a domicile restriction, this is usually a bad idea. If the party with the child decides to move far away with the child after the divorce (perhaps years later) the other party will regret not getting a domicile restriction up front in the decree. You should always try to get this restriction, especially since the court would usually order it anyway if you went to court. If you agree to go without one, and later you decide you really don't want your ex-spouse moving a long way away with your child in order to take that new job or to get married, you may be out of luck in court.

If you use a domicile restriction, you should always use a political boundary that can be seen on a map. Usually the restriction is to the county of the divorce and surrounding (contiguous) counties. If a party wants to move farther away at some point in the future, they will have to file a motion with the court asking for permission, which the court will may grant or deny depending on the situation. Another option is that one parent can move away, but they may have to leave the child with the party who is staying in the county. Any changes to domicile restriction that the parties want to make after the divorce can be made by an agreed modification order signed by both parties, or by court order after a hearing.

Cut the Kid a Break: Federal Tax Exemption for the Children

Unless the parties agree otherwise, the person who has the right to designate the primary residence of the child also has the right to claim the federal income tax exemption for the child. Consult your tax professional to see what arrangement makes sense for you.

Sometimes it makes sense for the person paying child support to get the exemption if they are making more money and therefore paying more taxes. You can also agree to split up the exemption by trading it back and for each year or giving each party the exemption related to a certain child if you have multiple children.

You Gotta Pitch In: Child Support

Financial responsibilities regarding the child are divided between the parents at divorce. The non-primary conservator (usually the dad) is responsible to feed, clothe and house the child only when they have possession of the child. The primary conservator (usually the mom) has primary responsibility to feed, clothe and house the child at all other times. If the child has financial needs beyond those, they usually will be the responsibility of the primary conservator to pay for them (costs for extracurricular activities, school books, etc.).

The financial obligations of the non-primary conservator are:

1.   House, clothe and feed the child when in their possession;
2.   Pay one-half the uninsured healthcare expenses for the child;
3.   Pay for health insurance for the child; and
4.   Pay child support.

That's it.

The parents can agree in the decree that no one has to pay child support. However, keep in mind that many judges will question this arrangement and ask you why you think this is in the best interest of the child (for example, where the primary conservator makes a lot more money than the non-primary conservator). The court may order child support anyway, even if the parties don't think it is necessary. If you are the primary (the child lives with you by default) you may wish you had that extra money in the future in order to help your child.

Also remember that child support can be adjusted a number of times after the divorce, even if initially the parties agreed to no child support. The primary conservator can come back to the judge and explain why they need to start child support now, and the court may order it. Also, child support can be increased (or decreased) by the court (upon request by one of the parties) based on changes in the income of the person paying the support.

Also note that the person paying child support has absolutely no control over how the other parent uses that money and the Texas courts have ruled that the paying spouse has no right to find out how it is used, either. By the same token, the parent receiving child support can use the money however they see fit and they do not have to explain how it was used to the other parent.

Calculating the amount of child support is easy thanks to the support guidelines set up by the Texas legislature in the Texas Family Code. Judges use these guidelines because they are easy to apply and give predictable outcomes. Although these are called guidelines, it is pretty much automatic that the court will follow them exactly.

The first step is to determine how much the person who will pay support earns per month. If the person's income varies due to commissions and bonuses, the court may use past earnings as a guide. The court may also determine how much the person should be earning if they are currently intentionally unemployed or intentionally underemployed. The court will, at a minimum, assume you could get a full-time job at minimum wage and calculate and order child support based on that even if you are currently unemployed (meaning you will have to go out and find a job and start paying support).

From the gross monthly earnings, you subtract what you pay for income taxes and social security (or what the Texas Attorney General says you should be paying for those items), which leaves you with net income. Note that the legislature has set a cap on net income of $8,550.00, so if the net income is more than that, you reduce it to $8,550.00.

Next you multiply the net income by the guideline percentage depending on how many children there are. The percentage is 20% for 1 child, 25% for 2, 30% for 3, etc. The percentage tops out at 40%. (The percentages are different if you have other children by another relationship that you are financially responsible to support through a court order.) The number you are left with is your monthly child support obligation.

One for You, One for Junior: Child Support Withholding

Since sometimes people ordered to pay child support don't pay, most courts will require that a withholding order be submitted along with the divorce decree, which will order the employer of the person paying support to withhold it directly from their pay. This is convenient if you are a salaried employee. However, if you are self-employed it doesn't really make sense.

Also, some divorcing couples do a withholding order, but put language in the decree that the order will not be submitted to the paying party's employer unless that person gets behind in his child support payments.

Texas Lends a Hand: The State Disbursement Unit

All child support in Texas now goes through the State Disbursement Unit of the Texas Attorney General Child Support Division. The check you pay in child support goes to this unit, which then issues another check to the recipient.

This system protects both parties because it generates a record of whether or not, and how much, child support was paid each month. It also insures that the other party received the money. If there is ever a dispute about these amounts, you can obtain a complete record of the payment history from the State Disbursement Unit.

An Apple a Day: Health Insurance

If left up to the court, the judge will always order that the person paying child support also pay for health insurance for the child. You can cover them under your own policy or, if your spouse's policy is better or cheaper, you can cover the child with that and reimburse the other party for that portion of the premium that covers the child. You can also agree to have the person receiving support responsible for paying the premium.

Note that these provisions do not provide health insurance for the parents. If you are covered under your spouse's health insurance plan, that will end after your divorce is final. You should ask the insurer about COBRA coverage, which allows you to remain covered for a certain period of time after the divorce, but at your own expense.

Just in Case: Life Insurance

It is a good idea for both parents to have life insurance for the benefit of the children. Otherwise, if the person paying support dies the child support will not get paid and the remaining parent is in a financial hole. Similarly, if the person receiving child support dies, the remaining person suddenly has the child full-time, with all the increased expenses associated with this change, while still earning the same income. Even though the parents got divorced (and may not like each other very much), they usually agree that they should have insurance set up like this to protect the child.

Note that if you already have your spouse named as the beneficiary of a life insurance policy (or of items in a will, or of a retirement account), once you get divorced those designations are automatically void. This can create a real problem if there is no backup beneficiary, since the court will hold the money until the child reaches 18. In the meantime, unless the remaining parent hires a lawyer, goes to court and gets permission to use the money to benefit the child, they will have no access to the money. Even worse, when the child reached 18, they receive the money directly (and how many 18-year old kids do you think will use that money wisely?).

Even if you make the beneficiary of the insurance money a trustee for the benefit of the child, it makes it difficult for the remaining parent, who has to get permission from someone else every time they want to use the money to benefit the child.

The way to avoid these problems is to rename the ex-spouse as the beneficiary of the insurance AFTER the divorce is finalized. Your attorney can help you put language in the decree requiring that each spouse do this within a certain amount of time after the divorce is final.

How much insurance should you get? The answer is: at least enough to replace the child support that would otherwise have been paid. Talk to your financial advisor about how much insurance you should get to cover child support and other items like college for the child or paying off a mortgage. Once the divorce is final, it is also a good idea for each parent to revise their will to set up a trust for the children and also to change the beneficiary designation on any retirement accounts to insure the money goes into the trust for the benefit of the child.

The Handyman Divorce: Doing It Yourself

It's true. You could get some forms off the internet and try to do your divorce yourself. However, quite a few "do it yourself divorces" are done incorrectly and later there is a dispute regarding the terms and the parties end up back in court fighting to straighten out the decree. Couples with no significant assets and no children may be able to do the divorce themselves. However, especially with assets and/or children, it is worth it to divorce correctly the first time by getting the help of the right attorney for your case.

Now that you have a general idea how Texas divorce works, let's get specific about **your** case and the search for the right lawyer.

What is the truth about attorney advertising?

Looking for an attorney to help you with your divorce case can be an overwhelming experience. If you search the internet you will see hundreds of websites for attorneys claiming that they handle divorce cases. Many of these ads say the same things, such as "protect your rights", "get the settlement you deserve", "low cost divorce" or "aggressive trial lawyer". What exactly does all this mean? How do you go about telling these attorneys apart? Most importantly, how do you choose the right attorney for your case?

When you see "low cost divorce", remember that most divorce lawyers bill on an hourly basis. You have some control over how much you spend based on what issues you are able to resolve by negotiation with your spouse. However, you cannot control the actions of your spouse. If your spouse makes outrageous demands that you are unwilling to accept, you may have to fight for your rights in court, which will increase your legal expenses.

Also remember that your attorney will usually require you to pay fees associated with the divorce, such as the fee for filing the divorce petition and the cost of having your spouse served with that petition. Be sure and clarify exactly what bills you are responsible for with any attorney you are considering hiring, and have a written contract for representation, signed by you and the attorney, that explains their rate and what other fees you are responsible to pay.

Another thing to consider with an attorney advertising a "low cost divorce" is: how many "low cost" cases must that attorney handle per month in order to pay his overhead expenses, etc.? If the attorney is forced by his fee structure to handle too many cases at once, will he have adequate time to properly prepare your case?

When you read such phrases as "get the settlement you deserve", be wary of any attorney that promises you that it will be easy to get you lots of money or to win child custody in your case. Any attorney who promises you this is not telling you the truth, because no one can predict exactly what will happen ahead of time in either settling your case or taking it to trial. After a careful evaluation of your case, an attorney should give you their opinion of your chances of getting the outcome you want, but they cannot honestly promise a particular outcome. Remember also that the evaluation of the case is an ongoing process. The prospects for a case may change as new facts are discovered during investigation and preparation of your case. An honest, experienced attorney will usually admit that they have "lost" cases (received an outcome at trial other than what the client was requesting from the court) that they probably should have won and they have "won" cases (got exactly what the client wanted, or even more) that they probably should have lost. The attorney will also admit that they do not know exactly why this happened other than that lawsuits involve people, and people (including witnesses, judges and juries) are unpredictable.

If the attorney states that he is an "aggressive trial lawyer", find out exactly what this means. Does the attorney actually take cases to trial, or does he settle most of them, or refer them out to other attorneys if they need to go to trial? Also, what does "aggressive" mean? Every attorney should zealously represent their client, but if they are obnoxious to the opposing attorney, the opposing spouse, the judge or the jury, they may do more damage to your case than someone who treats everyone involved with courtesy and respect. Being effective is not the same as being rude. Remember, some jurors (and even some judges) already have in their minds a stereotype that often in a divorce, one of the parties may be an obnoxious, dishonest opportunist. At the very least, they may suspect that either you or your spouse are lying regarding important issues in the divorce. If you or your attorney's demeanor reinforces this stereotype, you may have a problem. If the judge or the jury does not like and believe you or your attorney, they will usually find a way to make you lose.

The reputation of your attorney is important in that opposing attorneys respect attorneys that thoroughly prepare and are willing to take cases to trial. Therefore, it is important to have an attorney that is willing and able to take your case to trial when necessary.

It is important to remember a few other things when looking at attorney advertising. First, remember that anyone can buy an ad or create a website. A large, expensive ad or website does not necessarily mean that the attorney is the right one for you, or even a very good attorney. The attorney may be competent, but it is important that you check out their credentials and talk with them about how they will approach your case before you decide to hire them. Also, protect yourself by insisting on a written contract for representation.

Also, make sure that they are not an advertising "mill" that takes way too many cases, and then, if they need to go to trial, farms them out to other attorneys. You should know up front what attorney will be handling your case all the way through, and that your attorney is willing and able to try the case if necessary.

Finally, make sure the attorney's personality matches yours, since you are going to be working together for a while. To be successful in resolving your case it is important for you and your attorney to work as a team.

How do you find the right attorney for your case?

You should review your case with an attorney you are considering hiring for your case before you actually hire them. The attorney should be able to explain to you, clearly and concisely, how the divorce process works. They should also be able to explain to you the procedure if your case goes to trial. The attorney should give you give you a realistic assessment of your case and of your chances of achieving your desired outcome. You should feel comfortable dealing with the attorney, because you will need to communicate with him or her quite a bit during the course of your case.

The law related to divorce has its own unique requirements and potential pitfalls. Therefore, it is important to find an attorney that deals with divorce cases on a regular basis, and who is willing to take them to trial when necessary. Understand that the attorney on the other side usually knows which attorneys go to trial and which attorneys settle everything, and this affects their thinking as they evaluate whether to settle your case and how much they recommend their client to give you, both financially and regarding child custody issues.

The following steps will help jump-start your attorney search:

1.   Ask an attorney or someone else you know and trust to give you a referral to someone who handles divorce cases.

2.   Ask an acquaintance who has used a divorce attorney and is happy with their result to give you a referral.

3.   Check out the internet and do some Google searches, paying attention to client reviews.

4.   Before you talk to the attorney, ask if they have a booklet of information like this one or a web site that you can go to for more information about their methods for handling cases, their experience and their qualifications.

5.   Be wary of any attorney that pressures you to sign a contract quickly. If you need time to consider what to do, the attorney should give you time to review the contract at home in a relaxed setting before you make the decision about hiring an attorney.

6.   Do not hire any attorney who contacts you, trying to get you to hire him for a particular case. An attorney may send you information or contact you if you request it, but Texas has strict rules regarding attorneys, or anyone working on behalf of an attorney, who solicit clients (i.e. contacts the client before the client contacts them) either by telephone, in person or in writing.

7.   Before hiring an attorney, make sure you understand how you will be kept informed of your case's progress. Your attorney should explain the estimated timeframe for the case and be happy to answer questions via telephone or e-

mail. You should be able to arrange a telephone or in-person conference with the attorney when needed.

8.   Be sure and find out who will actually work on your case. Some things can be handled by legal assistants. However, if you are hiring an attorney because you like and trust them and believe in their skills, you want to make sure that is the person who is actually going to negotiate with the other side and, if necessary, try your case.

What are the typical steps in a divorce?

While every case is different, and not all cases require each of the steps outlined below, this is a list of the typical steps in preparing, and, if necessary, trying your divorce case.

Initial client interview: evaluate the client's claim, educate client regarding the legal process for divorce cases, determine any deadlines that apply.

Contact the opposing party or their attorney, giving them notice of representation.

File the divorce petition and serve the opposing party or answer the divorce petition filed by the opposing party.

Where appropriate, serve discovery requests (formal requests for documents and other information regarding assets, debts, child custody issues, history of the opposing party, etc.) on the opposing party or their attorney.

Answer any discovery requests served by the opposing party.

Gather all evidence related to the case, including assets, debts, marital history and child custody issues.

Interview witnesses, if appropriate.

Obtain testimony from the opposing party and any other witnesses as necessary via deposition.

Analyze the legal issues related to the case, including finances and custody.

Prepare for any temporary orders needed to govern the conduct of the parties while the case is pending and conduct a hearing regarding such orders if necessary.

Prepare for and participate in mediation to try and settle the case.

If mediation is unsuccessful, set the case for trial.

Prepare exhibits to be used at trial.

Prepare and file any necessary briefs and motions with the court.

Prepare the client and any witnesses for trial.

Try the case before a judge or jury

Review the verdict to see if either party has grounds for appeal.

Advise the client as to whether or not they should appeal the case.

Now let's look at these steps in a little more detail.

How do you start the divorce process?

A divorce is a civil lawsuit, and it begins like any other civil lawsuit. Your lawyer prepares a **"petition"** asking for a divorce. They file this petition with the court clerk's office in the appropriate county. Then, they either have the opposing party served with **"citation"** or they have them sign a **"waiver of citation"** accepting the lawsuit.

If the other side files the suit and serves the petition on you, your lawyer prepares an **"answer"** which they file with the court clerk and then serve on the opposing party. It does not matter who files for divorce first and there is usually no advantage in being the "first one to the courthouse" (unless the divorce may be filed in more than one county and you have a preference). However, remember that once you are served, you must file an answer within a certain time in order to prevent the other side from seeking a **"default judgment"** against you.

The parties usually will need **"temporary orders"** to be entered with the court to govern their behavior while the divorce is pending. These orders can be negotiated by the parties and their attorneys, or the court may hold a hearing to determine the terms of the order.

What happens after the lawsuit is filed?

After a lawsuit is filed, both sides may send each other **"discovery"** requests (mentioned earlier). You may serve formal discovery requests on the other party along with your petition or your answer, which must be answered by the opposing party within a certain amount of time. These are written questions about assets, debts, children issues, marital and other history of the parties and requests for documentation related to all of the above. Each side is allowed to discover what the other side will say at trial and their legal theories of the case. The opposing attorney usually will be permitted to see your mental health history, criminal history (if any), your work history, your financial history and your marital history. You may also have to give sworn testimony at a deposition. You are allowed to find out all of the above information about the opposing party as well.

After discovery is complete, the lawyers normally schedule the case for mediation (mentioned earlier) to see if it can be resolved without a trial. Mediation is voluntary, although most counties order you to attend mediation before you set the case for a final trial.

If mediation is unsuccessful, the parties set the case for court and a trial is held before either a judge or jury. After the trial is over, the parties review the result to determine is an appeal is recommended.

Wrapping up

While divorce can be painful and frightening, many people have a great "next phase" of their life after it is over. I hope the information in this book helps you understand the Texas divorce process so you can get through it and get on with your life.

For more information or to get help with a divorce or other family law matter please visit our website at **davidtoddlaw.com** or call us at **(512) 472-7799**.

About the author

David Todd is Board Certified in Family Law by the Texas Board of Legal Specialization. He has been representing Texans in divorce and other family law matters since 1989. To learn more visit davidtoddlaw.com.

David Todd, Attorney at Law
Todd Law Firm, PLLC
3800 N. Lamar Blvd., Suite 200
Austin, Texas 78756
(512) 472-7799
davidtoddlaw.com